In Control:
Learning to Say No to Sexual Pressure

Sexual pressure can be confusing and scary.

In Control:

Learning to Say No to Sexual Pressure

by Anna Kreiner

THE ROSEN PUBLISHING GROUP, INC.
NEW YORK

Published in 1997, 1999 by The Rosen Publishing Group, Inc.
29 East 21st Street, New York, NY 10010

Revised Edition 1999

Library of Congress Cataloging-in-Publication Data

Kreiner, Anna.
    In control : learning to say no to sexual pressure / Anna Kreiner.
      p. cm. — (The teen pregnancy prevention library)
    Includes bibliographical references and index.
    Summary: Discusses different kinds of sexual pressure and
  considers ways young people can negotiate with their partners and
  determine their own values and ethics regarding sex.
      ISBN 0-8239-2996-5
      1. Sexual ethics for teenagers—Juvenile literature.
    2. Teenagers—Sexual behavior—Juvenile literature. 3. Peer
    pressure in adolescence—Juvenile literature. [1. Sexual ethics.
    2. Youth—Sexual behavior. 3. Peer pressure.] I. Title.
    II. Series.
    HQ35.K68 1996
    306.7'0835—dc20   95-40057
CIP
AC

Manufactured in the United States of America

Contents

Introduction

***CHERYL AND JOSH** had been good friends for many years. Recently they started going out, and though they have kissed, they haven't done anything else. When they were just friends, they often spoke about not having sex until they were married. Now that they are falling in love, Josh has a different idea about the whole thing. Cheryl, however, still wants to wait.*

Vincent and César have been friends for years. They both have a crush on a girl named Wi Ling, whom they go to school with. Even though neither of the boys has actually gone out with her, they told their friends that Wi Ling was "easy." Why did they lie, and what will Wi Ling do when she finds out that they are spreading rumors?

Having a boyfriend or girlfriend in your teen years can be very exciting. Having a guy or a girl notice you makes you feel special. You are probably experiencing new feelings that are wonderful at times and frustrating at other times.

Part of any new intimate relationship is experimenting, including snuggling, holding each other and kissing.

Anything beyond this point can become a question of sexual pressure. Your boyfriend or girlfriend may be pressing you to go to the next step: one step further than you want to go, or further than you know is right for you at the time being. You are the only one who can define what "too far" means for you. You set the boundaries. You decide how physically intimate you want to become.

We all know today that engaging in sex can lead to anything from pleasure to deadly consequences; these should be understood before you are involved in any type of compromising situation. The first step is educating yourself to these potential dangers.

Do not wait until you are in a full sexual relationship to begin thinking about these consequences. Make any and all choices based on what is best for you. Abstinence (deciding not to have sexual intercourse) is the only absolutely sure way to prevent the sexual transmission of AIDS and to avoid other STDs (sexually transmitted diseases) and pregnancy. Practicing safe sex reduces these risks, but it does not eliminate them. However, if you have already had unprotected sexual intercourse, it is not too late to choose to be abstinent. The key word here is control. You are the only one who knows how you feel about this. You are the only one who can say *no*, It is up to you to respect yourself and uphold the personal values and goals you have set.

In fact, it would be useful to start thinking about these issues now, before you start experiencing sexual pressure. Anyone who is thinking about becoming involved in a relationship should consider these important questions:

• How far are you willing to go sexually?
• How would your family and friends feel about your choosing to be sexually active?
• Will you lose your partner if you say no?
• What will happen if you say yes to sex?
• Are you ready to become a parent?
• What about the risk of STDs such as AIDS (for which there is no cure)?

Think about these issues before you start to date or enter into a relationship. It is very important that you are clear about your point of view on sex, and it is easier to figure out that point of view before you start experiencing sexual pressure. If you choose not to have sex, it is important for your partner to respect your choice. He or she needs to understand that if you say no, you mean it; your partner should not expect that you will say one thing and do another. For both guys and girls, most of the pressure is off once a person definitely decides that sex is not what he or she is "into" at this time.

Sexual pressure comes in many forms. This book will help you to recognize sexual pressure and learn how to say no to it.

Peer pressure wears many different faces, and dealing with sexual pressure is a challenge. You may feel as if others will look down on you for saying no, or you may think that your partner will reject you. But there are many ways to say no and maintain both your relationship and your self-esteem.

You can still enjoy and look forward to dating without sexual pressure. In fact, without the pressure, you will probably have more fun. You certainly won't suffer any of the negative side effects of sexual activity, such as pregnancy, disease, stress, anger at yourself for giving in to something you don't believe in, or even contracting HIV. You will also know that a person is seeing you for who you really are and not for what you have to offer him or her sexually. All of this is because you made the decision to set your own boundaries, and you stuck to that decision.

Teens may be more likely to put sexual pressure on their partners if their friends make fun of them for not having sex.

1 Clarifying Your Values and Setting Boundaries

*"**I LOVE MY BOYFRIEND, BUT I KNOW THAT IF WE** have sex before both of us are ready, our relationship will suffer. I just don't want to risk getting pregnant right now," says Erin. "I'm not emotionally ready for that yet. My sister gave birth to her first child before she finished high school, but that's her and not me."*

"I think it's cool to be a virgin until you get married," says Maia. "It's so romantic. I want to save myself for my husband, and I don't feel that I need to defend my choice. The guys I go out with know the way I feel because I tell them that they can take it or leave it. It's also a good way to weed out the ones who are truly interested in me from those who just want to score."

"Those advertisements and television talk shows can't all be wrong about AIDS and sexually transmitted diseases," says Nori. "I am not willing to take that risk with my life, no matter how great it would be to have sex. Several minutes of pleasure is not worth giving up your life."

How do you feel about your own sexual behavior? What is important to you? What do you think is appropriate in a relationship?

Think about your values—your beliefs about what is right and wrong—before you get involved. Then you can make decisions that will feel right to you.

Many people believe that sex outside of marriage is wrong. You may have grown up in a family with strong religious beliefs. Many of these families think teens should wait until they are married before they have sex.

But many teens from nonreligious families also think that having sex now is not right for them. They have chosen sexual abstinence. People who are abstinent do not engage in sexual intercourse.

When you are a teenager, you go through many physical and emotional changes. You are still learning about your body and your relationships with other people. For many teens this is a time of exploration, and they are not yet ready to have sex.

Is It Worth It?

Sexual intercourse can be a healthy part of a committed relationship between mature, responsible people. Many people choose to put off having that special experience until they are sure they have found the right person. They decide to wait until

Risky sexual activity can lead to pregnancy and sexually transmitted diseases.

Some teens meet in discussion groups to encourage each other to remain abstinent.

they are in a long-term relationship or are married before they engage in sexual activity.

You may think that your current boyfriend or girlfriend is the person you will be with forever, but feelings can change. The person you are dating now may not be the person you marry or decide to stay with for the rest of your life. So this may not be a good time for you to get involved in serious sexual activity, especially considering the possible consequences of unsafe sexual practices: sexually transmitted diseases (STDs), including AIDS, and unwanted pregnancy.

"My twin sister got pregnant when she was four-teen," says Lamaine. "Our mother, who should have been enjoying her retirement years, had to help raise the

baby because May was too young to get a full-time job. The baby's father just disappeared. Up until the birth, he was around a lot, but then he split. He said he couldn't handle how the baby changed their relationship. From May's experience, I decided that I didn't want to have sex until I finished school."

"My boyfriend said that I would not get pregnant if we had sex only once," says Roxie. "Boy, was I a fool to listen to him. Now I'm pregnant and he's dating someone else. I want nothing to do with him. I don't believe in abortion, but I don't want a baby right now."

"This girl at school can get any guy she wants," says Chris. "She asked me out and we had sex even though I didn't want to. She said that my friends had done it, so why not me? Now I have herpes. Pressure sucks!"

The idea of having sex may be exciting, but you should remember that sex can complicate a relationship. You are taking on a new responsibility. It is important to think about the effects of your actions before you make any decisions about sex.

Sexual activity can have physical consequences. You run the risk of contracting many serious sexually transmitted diseases—such as chlamydia, gonorrhea, herpes, syphilis, or AIDS—by having unprotected sex. AIDS is a fatal disease for which

Staying within your boundaries might mean meeting your dates at public places.

there is no cure. It is passed from an infected person to someone else by the exchange of bodily fluids such as semen, blood, and vaginal secretions.

Even if you have sex only once or only during certain times of the month, you or your partner could get pregnant. You can get pregnant the first time you have sex.

You may not know your partner's sexual history. If you become sexually involved with this person, you are taking a major risk. Are you willing to take that risk? The only way you can be sure of avoiding the consequences of sexual activity is by being abstinent.

We have mentioned only a few reasons why

some people choose not to have sex. Do you have other reasons for not engaging in sex?

Once you know what is important to you, you will be able to make wise decisions about your sexual behavior. The first step is to determine clearly in your mind what you think is appropriate.

Setting Boundaries

Once you have established your values, you should set your boundaries.

How far are you willing to go sexually? Some teens are comfortable with holding hands. Eventually you may want to hug and kiss. It's normal to have feelings of affection for your boyfriend or girl-friend and to want to express them. But there are ways to do this without "going all the way."

It is a wise idea to talk with your partner about your boundaries. If each of you has a clear under-standing of how far you are willing to go, you will be less likely to encounter sexual problems later.

Dunja and Kal have been going out since last summer. Kal is popular and hangs out with a group of guys who like to party. Dunja is into sports and is trying to get a scholarship to college. "Even though we have talked about it a lot, Kal still doesn't respect the fact that I want to wait to have sex," says Dunja. "As much as I care about Kal, I can't continue having a relationship with someone who doesn't have the same values as I do. If we can't see eye-to-eye about something as important as sex, then how will we be able to make other important decisions in the future?"

"I have been playing music since I can remember," says Amelia." "When I met Julio last month and found out that he was also into music, I thought he was the perfect guy for me. We disagree on only one thing—sex. Julio is five years older than me, and he's been sexually active since he was fourteen. As much as I love him, I don't feel ready to have sex with him or anyone else right now. He doesn't get mad about it, but I am afraid he will go out and find someone else to date. I don't know what to do, especially since my parents are very conservative and don't believe in premarital sex.

From these scenarios you can see that each couple is facing a difficult situation. The most important thing to remember is that the decision to have sex is yours, and yours only. As with any relationship, honesty and good communication are essential. And whenever two people are involved, it is probable that there will be more than one point of view on any given topic. You should be comfortable expressing your own point of view, and you should expect to have it treated with respect. If someone you are involved with is unwilling to honor your opinion on any matter pertaining to your health, wellness, and/or your future, he or she is not a good partner for you.

People who truly love one another care about each other's points of view and concerns. It is very exciting to find someone with whom you can openly discuss things that are important to you both. When this occurs and you are not under any sexual pressure, you can establish a wonderful relationship that will bring lasting and fulfilling memories.

Set your limits before you get involved in a relationship. Sometimes in the heat of the moment, it is hard to think clearly. You may love being with your partner. But remember that your actions will have consequences. Think carefully before you engage in sexual activity.

If you set your limits early in the relationship, you won't have to worry about mixed signals later. And you can be sure of maintaining your values even when you are faced with sexual pressure. Learning to say no will help you stay in control.

2 Kinds of Sexual Pressure

One night Sean and Jan went to a football *game together. After the game Jan started to kiss Sean as they were walking back to the car. "I like it when Jan kisses me," says Sean. "Sometimes I want to be more sexually intimate with her, but that's not the way I was brought up."*

For the first few months that they were together, Jan teased Sean a lot and was a real flirt. "I tried hard to pressure him into sleeping with me, but he just kept on saying no, so I finally gave up on him."

"There's a guy named John in my computer class, and I think he's really cute," says Emilina. "He always wears this cool black leather jacket. One day he invited me to his house after school and he let me try on his jacket. We kissed for a while, but then he got really excited and I got scared and told him to stop. John said that if I sleep with him, he'll be my boyfriend forever. Now I'm confused. Maybe I'll give in and just give him what he wants. It would be nice to have a boyfriend."

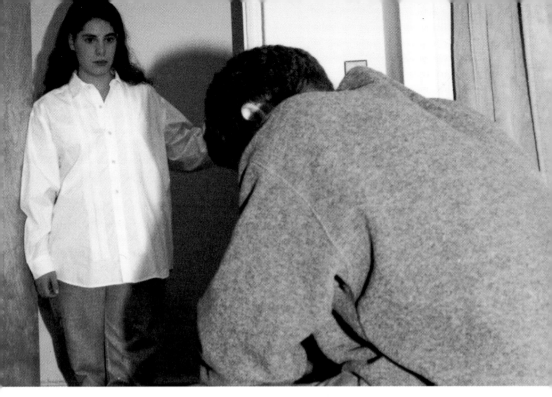

Some teenagers confuse sex with love, and get hurt when the relationship ends.

"It's Jennifer's birthday tonight," says Laz. "I'm taking her out to dinner, and I borrowed my uncle's truck. I even went to the drugstore and bought a box of condoms. I figure we'll just do it in the truck when I drive her home. It would be nice to wait until we're married, but I can't take the pressure from the guys at school."

Sexual pressure can take many forms. Anytime someone tries to get you to do something sexually that you don't want to do, he or she is exerting sexual pressure. All sexual pressure is inappropriate. If it makes you uncomfortable, it is wrong. Both guys and girls can exert sexual pressure. Some guys feel that they have to have sex "to be a

Giving in to a partner's pressure not to use birth control can put you at risk for pregnancy.

man." Some girls think having sex will prove their partner really loves them. Sex doesn't equal love. You can still be with and love your partner without doing anything that makes you uncomfortable.

Verbal Sexual Pressure

Some sexual pressure is verbal. Your partner may try to talk you into having sex. But don't let words like "please" make you think that you are being unfair for saying no. If you find yourself arguing with your partner about sexual involvement, it's not a good sign. The decision to have sex is a decision between two people. It is not healthy if you feel you have "given in" to your boyfriend's or girlfriend's desire to have sex.

Your friends may tell you that you should go to bed with your partner. But you're the one who will live with your choice and deal with the consequences—not them.

Pressure Not to Use Birth Control

"Come on, baby," Marco told Lucia. "You said you wanted to have sex. We don't need birth control. Condoms are a drag. I'll make sure you don't get pregnant."

Your partner may try to persuade you not to use birth control, saying that sex is better without it.

You may hear excuses like "It's no fun for me with a condom." Your partner may even try to make *you* feel bad by saying something like, "Don't you think I'm clean? I don't have any diseases!" or "Don't you trust me?"

But unprotected sex can be very dangerous. You may get a sexually transmitted disease, such as AIDS. And there is always the risk of pregnancy, even the first time a couple has sex.

No matter what your partner says, if you do decide to be sexually active, it is vital to protect yourself. Don't let your partner pressure you into having unsafe sex. If someone doesn't care enough about you to protect you from pregnancy and disease, do you really want to become sexually involved with him or her?

Women and men should consult a doctor or counselor to learn about birth control options. The condom is the only form of birth control that prevents against the transmission of sexually transmitted diseases such as AIDS. It protects against the transmission of HIV, which causes AIDS. But if you are sexually active, it is also important to take other precautions to prevent pregnancy. Women may choose to use the birth control pill, the diaphragm, the female condom, Norplant, Depo-Provera, the cervical cap, or spermicidal jellies and foams to provide additional protection. The most effective

Don't let your boyfriend or girlfriend use mind games to change your decision about sex.

protection against pregnancy—besides sexual absti-nence—is provided when the condom is used with another method of birth control.

Mind Games

Dean and Holly were in Dean's basement watching a video while lounging on his mom's comfortable purple couch. Holly was kissing Dean. She moved closer to him until she was almost lying right on top of him. "Come on, Dean," she coaxed. "We have been together forever. Aren't you ready for more than kissing and holding me? You know, you have friends who would trade places with you in a minute," she said.

Dean replied, "Holly, I have told you before that I

think you are beautiful and smart, but I don't want to do it with you or anyone else right now. I want to concentrate on my studies and on winning the math prize. I don't like this pressure you are putting on me to have sex—something has to give!" he exclaimed, pushing her off.

Later that night after Holly went home, Dean called his older brother for advice. After he had explained the situation, Mitch thought for a while and then replied, "Dean, don't let Holly pressure you."

"You're right," said Dean "but what if she decides to have sex with another guy?"

"It's important to stay true to your dreams and goals and not to get carried away by someone's demands on you," Mitch cautioned. "Don't allow anyone or anything to sidetrack you from your priorities. You just have to stay strong, man."

"You're right. Thanks for the advice," said Dean.

When Dean and Holly met up the next day, Dean explained that if Holly continued to threaten him that she would sleep with other guys, he would end their relationship."

In the end Holly apologized and said that she would stop playing games with him. She had never thought that he would threaten to break up with her.

"Oh, Dean," she said. "I guess I just thought that by having sex, we would become even closer, but now I can see that maybe things don't work like that."

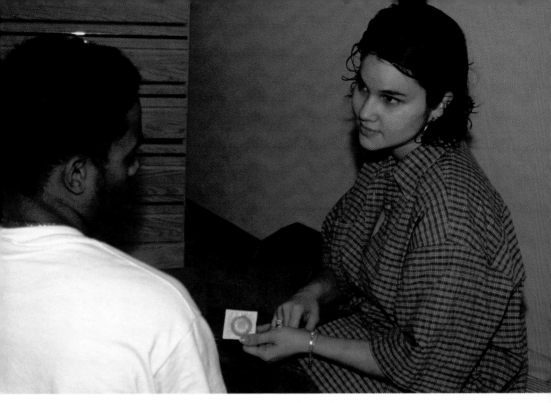
Girls can also put pressure on boys to have sex.

Sometimes people play "mind games" to get you to do what they want. For example, your boyfriend may say that if you love him you will have sex. But that isn't true. You can still love someone and not want to have sex. Sometimes the test of true love is being able to say no. And you will know that he loves you too if he is able to respect the boundaries you have established for yourself.

You always have the right to say no. If any sexual activity feels wrong, you can stop.

Your girlfriend may threaten to leave you if you don't have sex with her. That's another mind game. You don't have to do anything sexually that doesn't feel right. It is up to you to decide whether or not to continue the relationship. Do you want to stay with someone who makes you feel uncomfortable?

"Sally and I liked to walk on the beach at sunset. Usually we held hands. Sometimes we'd kiss good night," said Barry.

"But yesterday she started trying to unzip my pants. I'm not ready to get that close yet."

Physical Pressure

Sometimes sexual pressure becomes physical. Your boyfriend or girlfriend may start exploring your body. Your partner may try to take your clothes off or initiate more physical activity than you want.

You are the one who controls your body. If someone does something to you that you don't like, you have the right to say no.

You also have the right to change your mind. Just because you have sex once doesn't mean you have to have it again. You may decide you want to wait until you're older. And those feelings are perfectly legitimate. You're allowed to change your mind.

Unfortunately, sometimes sexual pressure can become violent.

Rape

Wendy was in tears. "I told him no a thousand times.

If you have been raped, it is very important to report the crime to the police and seek medical help right away.

One time, I said that I had changed my mind.
As soon as we started to have sex, I knew it was
wrong, and I told him so. But he wouldn't let me stop.
He just kept going. He said, 'You just said yes.
Now you're saying no. Don't you know what you
want?' "

No matter what—no always means no. No one has
the right to force you to have sex. Even if you
agreed at first, you have the right to change your
mind. If your partner forces you even after you
have said no—that's rape. Anytime you are forced
to have sex against your will, you are a victim of
rape. Rape is more than sexual pressure. It is a
crime. You have the right to report the person who
raped you to the police.

Rape is never your fault, no matter what you
were wearing or what you said or what you did.
Letting someone hold your hand or kiss you—even
going further—does not give him or her the right
to have sex with you.

It's important for you to get help if you have
been raped. You must report the incident to the
police. Talk to a counselor or find a support group.
No one deserves to be raped. If you are a victim of
rape, you may be frightened and angry. Other
people can help you to regain your self-esteem and
feel in control of yourself again.

"I let Mark come into my room so we could watch a movie," said Mira, a high school junior. "My parents were out for the night. I didn't think anything would happen because we've done this so many times before. But I was wrong. As soon as the movie started, Mark turned out the lights. Then he forced me to have sex. I begged him like crazy to stop, but he wouldn't."

Unfortunately, date rape is a common problem. Every year thousands of women are raped by men they know. Some men are also the victims of date rape. But many people are afraid to talk about it because they are embarrassed, or they think they deserved what happened to them. Rape is never your fault! Just because you know a person doesn't give him or her the right to have sex with you when you say no.

Even if you've had sex with your boyfriend or girlfriend before, it doesn't give him or her the right to expect sex from you. No matter what, the decision is always yours.

Kissing or fooling around doesn't automatically mean the next stage is sex. Don't let your partner pressure you into having sex "because we've gone this far." You always have the right to say no at any point.

If your partner tries to force you to have sex, you have the right to protect yourself. First try

Don't ruin a happy relationship just because your friends are telling you to have sex.

talking to him or her. If that doesn't work, you may need to be more assertive. Yell for help and try to run away. If you decide to fight, fight with all of your strength; getting away from the person, though, is still your best self-defense.

If you have been raped or had other force used on you, leave the location as soon as possible and get help by calling 911.

Many schools, community centers, and women's groups offer self-defense classes. You might consider enrolling in one of these programs so that you can better protect yourself if sexual pressure becomes physical or violent. *The Get Prepared Library of Violence Prevention for Young Women,* listed at the back of this book, shows you specific techniques for staying safe.

Peer Pressure

"All the girls I know said they couldn't wait to have sex with their boyfriends," said a high school junior.

"I don't want to have sex now. Holding hands and kissing are enough for me. But my friends will think I'm a baby if I don't go all the way. Maybe I should say yes to sex with my boyfriend."

Being a teenager can be a hard time socially. You want to have friends and fit in with the crowd. But having sex when you don't want it will probably make you feel bad about yourself and angry at the people who pressured you.

Dealing with peer pressure is a challenge. You may be afraid that no one will accept you if you don't have sex. But it's important for you to do what you think is right, no matter what.

Sometimes the peer pressure you feel may not even be based in reality. Listen to Ramon's story.

"All of the guys in the locker room used to brag about how they 'scored' with the girls on Saturday night," said Ramon. "But I kept my mouth shut. I thought I was the only one who had never slept with a girl.

"One night my friend Paul and I were talking about

girls. I trust him, so I asked him if I really was the only one who was still a virgin.

"Paul started to laugh. I was afraid he was laughing at me. But do you know what he told me?

"He said that most of the guys on the team hadn't ever slept with a girl. They were just bragging because they wanted to be macho."

You may think that everyone around you is having sex. But that's not true. Many other people your age have decided to say no to sexual intercourse. In a recent survey, 76 percent of the male teens said they thought it was okay to say no to sexual pressure.

Often teens who have had sex wish they had waited. Another survey found that 80 percent of sexually active teen males who were asked the ideal age to start having sex indicated an age older than they were when they first had sex.

The most important part of making sexual choices is to do what seems right for you. It doesn't matter whether or not any or all of your friends are getting involved sexually. The bottom line is that it's your body. Your friends have their own bodies—they shouldn't be telling you what to do with yours.

3 Why Do People Use Sexual Pressure?

SEXUAL PRESSURE IS NEVER RIGHT, NO MATTER what the reason for it. Knowing *why* people exert sexual pressure doesn't make it right, but it may help you figure out effective ways to say no.

Some people think that engaging in sexual activity will improve their relationship. But sexual pressure damages feelings of trust and respect. If you pressure your partner, you show that you don't really care about him or her. If you are not willing to respect your partner's boundaries, you are likely to upset him or her. Your partner may decide to leave the relationship. And even if your partner stays with you, he or she is not likely to feel very comfortable. In the long run, then, sexual pressure won't help you, your partner, or your relationship.

Some teenagers honestly feel that they are ready to have sex. They try to persuade their partners to go along with them—even if their partners don't want sex yet.

But some teens who exert sexual pressure don't

It may seem like everyone is having sex, but this is often not the case.

really want to have sex. They are responding to what they believe society expects of them. They think they have to act in a certain way sexually in order to fit in properly.

Often there are different expectations for males and females in our society. But many of these expectations are based on misinformation.

You should be able to distinguish the facts from the fiction. Then you can stay in control and say no to sexual pressure.

Gender Expectations

Both boys and girls may exert sexual pressure on their partners. But in a good relationship, each partner respects the other's boundaries. It is wrong for a boy to try to force his girlfriend to have sex. And it is just as wrong for a girl to try to persuade her partner to sleep with her if he doesn't want to.

Both boys and girls who believe the myth that "real men have sex" may use sexual pressure on their partners. How can you say no?

If you are a male, remember that being a "real man" doesn't mean you have to be sexually active. You don't need to do anything that makes you uncomfortable just to show you are a man.

You should never try to pressure your partner to have sex. She will not think you are macho if you make her uncomfortable; she is more likely to want to get out of the relationship.

Some girls also think that "real men have sex," and they may try to pressure their partners into having sexual intercourse. If you are a girl, remember that your boyfriend may not want to have sex. You have no right to try to make him act against his beliefs.

If he doesn't want to become close sexually, don't try to force him. You will not be doing anyone any good, and you are likely to put your relationship at risk if you keep pressuring him.

Are your friends bugging you about having sex? Are you afraid they will think less of you if they know you are abstinent? First of all, remember that many of them probably have not had sexual intercourse. And even if they have, you don't have to copy them.

You come first when you make decisions about your sexual behavior. It doesn't matter what anyone else thinks. You must live with yourself and the consequences of your actions.

Also remember that you don't have to discuss your sexual choices with your friends. Your decisions are your own business.

But if you do decide to talk with your friends, you can tell them that you are doing what feels right for you. True friends will respect you for making up your own mind and staying in control of your life. If your peers tease you or make jokes about your choices, they are not real friends. You can find other people who will respect your decisions.

Some men and women think that men and boys should be in control of a relationship. They believe that the male should determine how far both partners go. If you are a woman and you believe this, it may be hard for you to say no to sexual pressure. You may think you have to do what your partner says even if it makes you uncomfortable. And boys who think that men have more power may be more likely to put sexual pressure on their partners.

But this belief is false. Both partners in a relationship are equal. Both of you have a right to stay

It is important to realize that television and movies show sex between young people because "sex sells," not because it is what normal teenagers should do.

in control of your bodies. No man should force a woman to do anything that makes her feel uncomfortable sexually. And a woman always has the right to say no to any form of sexual pressure.

Sexual Pressure in the Media

The movies and television often show couples engaging in sex. This might lead you to think that "everyone is doing it." Prime-time television contains about three sexual acts every hour, usually between unmarried couples.

Television and movie producers include sex scenes because "sex sells." But what you see in the media often isn't realistic.

The characters frequently engage in unsafe sex. One study of daytime television found that fifty hours of programming included 156 sex acts—but mentioned safe sex or birth control only five times.

It is important to remember that television and movies make sex seem exciting, but they often leave out the consequences. In real life, sex isn't always glamorous. You may encounter other messages in the media, in your school, or at home. Before you accept and believe those messages, think about whether they are true. What are they saying about boys and girls and sexual pressure?

4 How to Say No and Stay in Control

"MARTA KEPT TRYING TO PUSH ME INTO HAVING SEX. I wanted to be with her, but I couldn't handle the constant pressure. I got tired of her trying to push me beyond where I felt comfortable," said Sam. "So I finally decided to get out of the relationship. I'm much happier now. Someday I'd like to have another girl-friend, but for now I'd rather be alone than be with someone who makes me uncomfortable."

"I really love Michael, but one thing about him drove me crazy," said a high school student. "We went to the movies together every Saturday. And every time we left he would try to get me to go home and go to bed with him.

"I thought a long time about my feelings and whether or not I wanted to stay with him. I talked to my mom and my sister. Finally I decided that I wanted to be with him, but only if he would respect my boundaries.

"We had a long talk, and he agreed to stop the pressure. I'm glad things worked out for us."

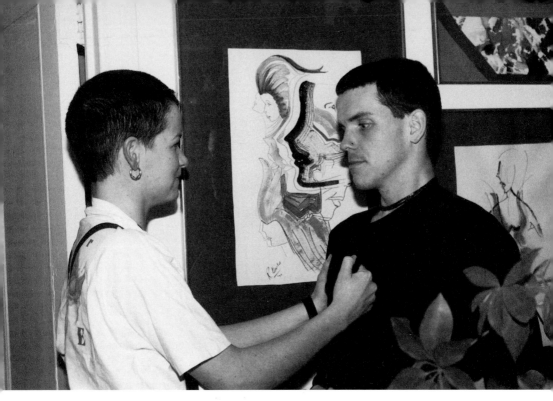

If your partner is not respecting your feelings, it is time to get out of the relationship.

"Sara and I have been dating for two months," said Tom. "I love to be with her. She's funny and smart, and we have a lot of interests in common. But about two weeks ago she started asking me to sleep with her. I'm not ready to be sexually active. And now I don't know whether I want to stay with her.

"On the one hand, I really enjoy spending time with her. We have fun together, and she makes me happy. I feel good about myself when I'm with her—or at least I did until she started the sexual pressure.

"I do wish we could continue our relationship. But I'll stay with her only if she stops the pressure. I'm going to talk to her and see how she reacts."

If your partner is putting sexual pressure on you, you need to decide whether or not to stay in the relationship.

How do you feel about your partner? Do you think he or she will respect your feelings?

What are the benefits of staying in the relationship? Your partner has probably become a very special person in your life. The two of you may have the same hobbies or interests. You enjoy spending time together—going to the movies, taking a walk, or just talking.

What are the disadvantages of staying? Does your partner's sexual behavior make you very uncomfortable? Is the sexual pressure starting to take over the good parts of your relationship? How much anxiety do you feel when you are with your partner?

If your partner makes you too uncomfortable, it is probably time for you to get out. But you may decide you want to try to work things out. If so, you need to figure out how to negotiate.

Before you approach your partner, it is important to be clear about what you want. Think about your values and your limits. If your partner is putting sexual pressure on you, make sure you know what is making you uncomfortable. The more definite you are about what you want, the better able you will be to communicate effectively and negotiate with your partner.

Techniques for Saying No

You know your values and have established your boundaries. You know what you need to say to your partner—now how do you say it?

The best approach is to be straightforward and direct. Setting your limits early will help you avoid trouble later. Talk to your partner about why you don't want to have sex. Explain how you feel. You don't have to lie or make excuses. Telling the truth is best. But even if you set your boundaries early, you may still encounter sexual pressure later.

"Ethan kept pressuring me to sleep with him," said Tanya. "Finally I couldn't stand it anymore. I decided that we had to sit down and talk or else I couldn't continue the relationship.

"I told him that he was making me very uncomfortable. I don't want to have sex now, and I couldn't really enjoy being with him anymore. The sexual pressure was making me too upset.

"I was surprised at his reaction. He told me he wasn't ready for sex yet either, but he thought I would think less of him if we didn't go all the way. Once we had discussed it openly, our relationship was much better. Neither one of us felt we were doing anything we didn't want to do. And Ethan was actually relieved. He knew he didn't have to put on an act or do anything that didn't feel right."

Being honest and direct is the best approach when dealing with sexual pressure.

"I was nervous about saying no to Lisa," said Gabriel. "She kept pressuring me and pressuring me. Finally I talked to my brother. He told me I should just tell her I wasn't ready. If she couldn't handle that, it was time for us to go our separate ways.

"I finally got up the courage to tell her how I felt. She was really angry and wouldn't talk to me for a while. But after a few weeks she called me on the phone. She told me she had thought about what I said, and she respected me for my choice. She still wants to have sex, but she knows I don't. So for now we're not going to sleep together."

If you want to go more slowly than your partner, tell him or her your limits. You might say, "I really like kissing you and hugging you. But that's as far as I'm willing to go. Anything more makes me uncomfortable." You should go at your own pace.

"I really like spending time with Wayne," said Allison. "And I like kissing him or holding hands. But I'm not ready to go further than that. When he tried to get me to go to bed with him, I was completely honest.

"I said, 'Wayne, I don't want to get pregnant or get AIDS. *And even if we use birth control, I'm just not ready to have sex yet. I want to wait until I get married.'*

"I thought Wayne would dump me, but he was

really cool about it. I think he understood how I felt, and he told me he was glad I explained how I felt. He said a lot of girls aren't so honest. They just sort of play along and send all kinds of messages. Then he doesn't know how to react to them."

Here are some ways you might explain to your partner why you are saying no:

- "I'm worried about getting AIDS or other diseases."
- "I'm not ready to be a parent yet, and I don't want to take the risk of becoming one."
- "I really like you, but sex isn't a priority for me right now. I want to wait until I'm older."
- "I want to make absolutely sure I'm ready, and I'm still deciding."
- "According to my religious upbringing, sex before marriage is wrong. I hope you can respect my beliefs."
- "My parents are really strict, and they'd kill me if they found out."

Avoiding Sexual Pressure

You can try to avoid getting into situations where sexual pressure is likely to get out of control. Stay away from parties where there is heavy drinking or drug use. Using alcohol and other drugs can impair your judgment and you may do things you

Drugs and alcohol can affect your ability to make good decisions.

wouldn't do if you were sober. This can lead to dangerous consequences.

- One study found that 80 percent of teen pregnancies occur after those involved have consumed drugs or alcohol at a party.
- A recent servey showed that an alarming 39 percent of males (and 18 percent of females) believe that it is okay for a boy to force sex upon a girl if she is under the influence of alcohol or other drugs.
- Another study found that sexually active teens who drink or use drugs use condoms 16 percent less often after drinking and 25 percent less ofter after using drugs.

- If current trends continue, 40 percent of this year's fourteen year-olds will become pregnant before they are twenty.
- A survey of college students found that 75 percent of the males and more than half of the females involved in date rape incidents had been drinking or using other drugs before the attack.

If you are on a date with someone new or who you don't know very well, it is a good idea to go to a place where there will be other people around, like a movie theater or a restaurant.

If you plan to attend a party where you don't know many of the guests, go with a friend so that the two of you can look out for each other.

Always let someone else know—whether it's your parents, a brother or sister, or a friend—when and where you are going on a date, and make sure that you have a way of getting home if you decide it's not working out. If you can't drive, call a relative, a friend, or a taxi. If you think you are in danger, contact the police right away.

Remember that you always have the right to say no to sexual pressure. Once you can do that, you will find that there are many advantages to being in control.

Staying in control will help you to feel strong and confident.

5 Being in Control Is Cool

"CHARLIE AND I DECIDED VERY EARLY ON THAT we wouldn't have sex at all," said Liz. "Now we have a chance to enjoy each other without worrying about anything else.

"We go to the movies or take walks together— and basically just hang out. I really like to be with him. I feel good about our relationship since we decided right away how we would handle the sex issue. Now we can concentrate on enjoying our time together instead."

Liz and Charlie have both decided to stay in control in their relationship. And they are gaining many benefits. Each of them established clear boundaries at the beginning of their relationship. Now they can be sure that they are doing what they want to do. Neither partner feels pressured, and they have the opportunity to enjoy the non-sexual aspects of dating.

Stu asked Pam to go to the junior prom. Pam was really excited—and scared. She had always been shy, and she hadn't dated much before. Pam was afraid Stu might not think she was experienced or exciting enough. She thought she might like to kiss him. But what should she do if he asked her to do more?

Stu and Pam had a great time at the dance. After they left the prom, Stu took Pam for a drive. He stopped the car and started to kiss her. Then he asked her if he could unbutton her dress.

"I was really nervous," said Pam. "I didn't want to go further sexually, and I was afraid he would get angry or just leave me by the side of the road. But I decided that I had to do what I felt was right. I told him that he had to stop.

"And you know what? He respected what I said. He didn't try to go any further.

"I really felt good about myself. I stayed in control that night. And we've continued to date.

"I'm glad I was able to say no. I have more confidence in myself. I know I can do what feels right for me, no matter what kind of sexual pressure anyone might try to put on me."

When you are in a relationship, you share a part of yourself with another person. But you should also be able to maintain your own identity and know what is important to you. When you can say

You may prefer to be alone rather than be with someone who makes you feel pressured.

no to sexual pressure, you remain in control.

Being able to say no improves your confidence and makes you feel better about yourself. You can get more enjoyment out of your relationship since you won't be doing anything you're not ready for. You won't resent your boyfriend or girlfriend for making you do something you don't want to do. And you won't be upset with yourself for making a mistake you'll regret later.

Your self-esteem will be high because of your ability to trust yourself. If you have self-confidence about your sexual choices, you know that you can also make good decisions in other areas of your life.

"It seemed like every guy I went out with expected me to sleep with him," said Alicia. "One guy even had the nerve to say that it was okay if I didn't sleep with him, but he planned to tell his friends that we had done it because they would think it was weird if we hadn't! I said that was crazy. If he didn't feel like it would be cool to go out with me unless we were sleeping together, then he wasn't going to have the honor of going out with me at all. I'm going to wait until the guys my age are more mature. Right now, none of them seem to be able to handle dating without sex.

"Since I made my decision not to date right now, I've had a lot more time and energy for other things,

like my interest in student government. I'm also able to spend more time with friends—both male and female. They all helped me to organize a campaign for student body president. I won the election by a landslide! I'm so busy now with my new responsibilities that I can't imagine having time for a boyfriend. The weird thing is, I'm getting asked out more than ever! But being alone is really giving me the chance to figure out who I am. When the right guy comes along and I do decide to date again, I'll be able to bring a lot more to the relationship."

Learning to say no to sexual pressure is a big step toward becoming a responsible adult. You have shown that you can make wise choices about what you think is best for you.

Sexual pressure is one of the most difficult things teenagers deal with. It's hard to turn someone down, especially when it's someone you really like. You may be made to feel that you're being uptight or a prude. This is only because the person is feeling defensive and insecure about his or her own actions. People who put sexual pressure on others are usually feeling some sort of pressure themselves. Remind your partner that sexual involvement carries many risks, both emotional and physical.

Giving in to sexual pressure before you're ready

may not seem like a big deal now, but it can get a lot more complicated if you contract HIV, the virus that causes AIDS, or another sexually transmitted disease, or if you find yourself faced with an unintended pregnancy. Being sexually intimate with someone before you're ready can also hurt your relationship, leaving you both feeling guilty, uncertain, even angry.

If you can say no to sexual pressure, you have an important tool for protecting yourself.

Your decisions about your sexual behavior now and in the future will be good ones because they will reflect what you think is important. And you will develop good relationships because you will be able to relate well with others while staying in control of your body and your life.

Glossary

abstinence The act of refraining from having sexual intercourse.

AIDS (Acquired Immunodeficiency Syndrome) Deadly viral disease that may be spread by sexual contact, intravenous drug use, or the exchange of bodily fluids, including blood, semen, and vaginal secretions.

contraception Methods of birth control; ways of avoiding pregnancy, including condoms, birth control pills, diaphragms, and other methods.

date rape (acquaintance rape) Forcible sexual intercourse carried out by someone who knows the victim. The criminal may be a boyfriend/girlfriend, an acquaintance, or a friend of the victim.

gonorrhea A sexually transmitted disease that causes a swelling of the genital mucous membranes.

herpes A sexually transmitted disease with symptoms that include clusters of blisters on the mouth, skin, or genitals.

peer pressure Attempts by friends, classmates, or acquaintances to persuade a person to engage in certain behavior.

prude A person who is unusually modest.

rape The act of forcing someone to have sexual intercourse against his or her will. Rape is a crime of violence.

sexual pressure Verbal or physical attempts to persuade someone to engage in sexual activity.

sexually transmitted disease (STD) One of several disorders, such as syphilis, chlamydia, gonorrhea, herpes, and AIDS, that a person can catch from a sexual partner.

Where to Go for Help

In the United States:

Advocates for Youth
1025 Vermont Avenue NW, Suite 200
Washington, DC 20005
(202) 347-5700
e-mail: info@advocatesforyouth.org

Bethany Christian Services Crisis Pregnancy Hotline
1120 Goffle Road
Hawthorne, NJ 07576
(800) BETHANY [238-4269]
Web site: http://www.bethany.org/1800bethany.html

Big Brothers/Big Sisters of America
230 North 13th Street
Philadelphia, PA 19107
(215) 567-7000
e-mail: national.bbbsa.org
Web site: http://www.bbbsa.org

Planned Parenthood Federation of America
810 Seventh Avenue
New York, NY 10019
(212) 541-7800
e-mail: communications@ppfa.org
Web site: http://www.plannedparenthood.org

Pregnancy Crisis Center Hotline
5500 Old Frederick Road
Baltimore, MD 21229
(800) 492-5530
Sexually Transmitted Disease Hotline
(800) 227-8922
Web site: http://www.cdc.gov

In Canada:

Bay Center for Birth Control
790 Bay Street, 8th Floor
Toronto, Ontario M5G 1N8
(416) 351-3700

Crisis Pregnancy Center
300-2445 13th Avenue
Regina, Saskatchewan S4P 0W1
(306) 757-3356
Web site: http://www.cableregina.com/nonprofits/
    cpcregina/index.html

Head and Hands Clinic
2304 Old Orchard
Montreal, Quebec H4A 3PA
(514) 481-0277; If busy, call: (514) 431-3643
    maliling address: P.O. Box 446, N.D.G. Station, Mon-
tréal, Québec, H4A 3P8

Planned Parenthood Federation of Canada
1 Nicholas Street, Suite 430
Ottawa, Ontario K1N 7B7
(613) 241-4474

For Further Reading

Bode, Janet. *Kids Still Having Kids: People Talk About Teen Pregnancy.* Franklin Watts, Inc., 1993.

Canfield, Jack (Ed.), et. al. *Chicken Soup for the Teenage Soul: 101 Stories of Life, Love, and Learning.* Health Communications, 1997.

Carlip, Hillary. *Girl Power: Young Women Speak Out.* Warner Books, 1995.

Englander, Annrenee (Comp.), *Dear Diary, I'm Pregnant: Teenagers Talk About Their Pregnancy.* Firefly Books, 1997.

Feller, Robyn M. *Everything You Need to Know About Peer Pressure.* Rosen Publishing Group, 1997.

Jukes, Mavis, Tilley. *It's a Girl Thing: How to Stay Healthy, Safe, and in Charge.* Alfred A. Knopf, 1996.

Kaplan, Leslie S. *Coping with Peer Pressure.* Rosen Publishing Group, 1999.

The Get Prepared Library of Violence Prevention for Young Women. 8 vols. New York: Rosen Publishing Group, 1995

Trapani, Margi. *Reality Check: Teenage Fathers Speak Out.* Rosen Publishing Group, 1999.

Index

About the Author

Anna Kreiner was born and raised in the Philadelphia area and received a master's degree in public health from the University of California at Los Angeles.

Photo Credits

Cover by Guillermina de Ferrari; pp. 27, 29 by Ira Fox; p. 42 by Yung-Hee Chia. All other photos by Guillermina de Ferrari.

Layout and Design

Erin McKenna